The Kaleidoscope of Poetry

1,100 Poem Challenge Vol 1

Stone Fauks

The Kaleidoscope of Poetry

The following is a collection of philosophy and poems written by the author from his experiences, studies, and creativity. Any similarities to any other works are purely coincidental.

STONE
FAUKS

#1100poems

Vol 1

Preface

When I was in school, the parents had the option to come up to the school to get our report cards or just have the children bring them home. My mother always concerned about my education would leave work early, come to my school, get my report card, and talk to my teachers. One day when I was in grammar school, after she got my grades and saw my reading score was the lowest in the class. I had an F in reading. My mother asked my teacher. What could she do to improve my grades? She didn't leave it to the teacher to do all the work, to teach me, to educate me. She took matters into her own hands. The teacher told her to read with me and have me read to her. After school that day we went to a store and bought some books, I don't remember what store, I don't even remember what books we bought, but I do remember us reading together that day. She would read to me, but most often I would read to her, anytime I mispronounce a word or had trouble with a word she would help me figure it out.

From there I developed a love for reading. I started with comic books and then onto Poetry, because they were short, even though not always easy to understand. Eventually I moved to short stories and novels.

I fell in love with reading so much so that I developed a desire to write. I was more interested in writing poetry because I felt I could express myself freer through poetry, than telling someone else's story.

From fourteen years old to my late thirties. I'd written hundreds of poems, and I had completed my first short story. After a big fight with my wife. I stayed with my mom for a few days, when I went back home, I couldn't find my writings anywhere, my wife said she didn't know where they were. I kept them in one place so I could easily find them. I checked the whole house and never found them. She never confessed to tossing them. I had become overprotective of my work.

I was always nervous about publishing my poetry, I was always self-conscious about people not liking what I wrote. Despite my fears

I entered contests and performed my poems on stage. I guess it was because the praise was instantaneous.

I saw a Facebook add for a self-publisher, I discussed it with my girlfriend, she told me to go for it, and she would help anyway she could. I contacted the publisher we discussed prices, and I selected 50 poems, formatted them, and sent them to the publisher.

A few months later I agreed to do an interview with Stu Taylor. I wasn't as nervous as I thought I'd feel. It was quick and exciting.

I continued writing poetry and I've started a few short stories. But I didn't push myself to do anything special. Surfing around Instagram and Threads I saw a few poets had done a poem a day for thirty days challenge. On YouTube I saw an influencer reacting to a young lady's work and he pointed out everything he thought was wrong with her books. I thought about how I had been around longer than her and I'm still unknown.

I decided I had to do something more with my writing I had to publish more.

The thirty-day challenge was good, but I felt that wasn't a good challenge for me. My original goal was to write one thousand poems in a year. After doing the math I realized if I did three poems it would come to 1,095 and I figured I could add five more to make it 1,100.

I started this challenge on September 1, 2024

These books are a collection of poems on various subjects.

This book is the third in a four-volume series each book will contain 275 poems. That will be three poems a day until August 27, 2025, when I will write four poems a day till the end of the month.

Which will give me the 1,100.

Thank you for your interest and support.

Stone Fauks

Challenge,
1,100 poems in 365 days

Starting this Sunday September 1st 2024 I'm giving myself a 365 day challenge. I'll be writing three poems a day every day until August 28th 2025 when I'll write four poems a day for the last 5 days of the challenge. The poems will be any length, any genre, and any style. Wish me luck as I start on this poetic journey.

STONE
FAUKS

I Don't Pray

I do not pray that God will
remove your obstacles,
but I do pray that he gives you
knowledge and courage to
overcome your trials.
I do not pray that everyone

will treat you kindly,
but I do pray that God will give
you discernment of those trying to
take advantage of and manipulate you.
I do not pray that God will give you wealth,
but I do pray that he will give you
wisdom on how to effectively
use your wealth.
(1)

Average Man

I am not the best man
I am an average man
doing the best he can
(2)

Growth Requires Death

Advancement can only come when
the outdated is destroyed.
A person cannot be wise and ignorant.
Either he will be active
And successful or lazy and poor.
As you age old cells die and
are replaced with new ones.
Growth, whether mental,
physical, social, or technological
requires death.
(3)

Karma

Being slick I stole a pen
Snuck it in my pocket knowing
it was forbidden
but thinking I had won
ignoring the hurt I had done.
When I pulled it out again
ink covered my hand.
The result of my crime
for everyone to see
All I feel now is guilty
(4)

Lazy

Ants search every day
Bees collect nectar daily
Lions hunt each day.
Even the sloth is busy day to day
it takes hours to gather and eat
Their food, but they get the job done.
Man wants to do less
than the sloth.
Many poets, philosophers, and
religious texts speak against being
idle, but for a lot of people being
lazy is the goal.
People think having millions of
dollars are a reason to be lazy
but the wealthiest people
stay busy, reading, learning,
working.
(5)

Success

Learn
Fail
Learn
Fail
Learn
Breakthrough
Learn
fail
Learn
grow
Learn
fail
Learn
Fail
Learn
Breakthrough
(6)

A Rose Bed

People say that "life is not a bed
of roses."
But I am beginning to think
that life is like a bed of roses.
You see all the pretty colors.
you smell the sweet fragrance.
But thorns are hiding underneath
waiting to prick, to stick, and to stab
you, waiting to cause injury.
Loss of a job, your spouse cheating,
kids getting hurt, mental, and physical
injuries are hidden beneath the fantasies
and dreams of the life you desire.
(7)

How Much is Enough

How much is enough?
A Mountain of gold,
a palace surrounded by guards,
your name a household word,
people kissing your feet telling
you how much they love you?
What void are you trying to fill,
what heartbreak are you trying to patch,
what appetite do you have that love
from one person cannot satisfy?
Will it take the love of the world
to appease you or just
one hug and kiss from someone
who loves you.
The emptiness you're trying to fill
can only be satisfied when you
learn to love yourself.
(8)

Members-Only

This is a Members-Only establishment.
The owner must invite you to join.
If you try to force your way in you will be
Forcibly ejected and not allowed reentry.
Further membership and visitor's passes
will be denied.
If you are allowed to enter and
you break any of the
following rules or regulations
the repercussions will
be the direct result of your infraction.
Lie once = warning
Lie twice = ejection from the premises
Cheat = ejection from premises
and membership revoked and
will never be reinstated
If you agree to these terms,
then you may proceed to apply
to become a member of my heart.
(9)

My Days Gets Better

My days gets better when
I see your smile
My days gets better whenever
You're around
My days gets better when
I see your sassy style
My days gets better when
I see the sparkle in your eyes
My days gets better when
I hold your hand
My days get better when
I see your smile
My days are gloomy when
You're not near
My saddest days are when
You're not here
(10)

Here and Now

Now smile through the tears.
Now smile through the hurt.
Now smile and be strong
Now smile though things seem hard
Now is just a moment in your life
You must be here to see the other side
I'm here when you need to vent
I'm here now.
(11)

One Spirit

Thinking of you, I drift into a dream
Dreaming of you, I want you near
Being with you, I want to hold you
Hugging you, I want your kiss
Kissing you, I want your love
Loving you, fills my heart
In my heart, we are one,
One being of intimacy
(12)

Living my best life
Requires knowledge planning,
Many sleepless nights
(13)

Choose the life you want
work towards it every day- it's
uncomplicated.
(14)

Eyes are two black pearls
Heart tender and full of love
Kissable, sweet lips
(15)

Monsters and Dragons

For many years I've wielded this sword and I'm still
unknown.
Many monsters and dragons
I've faced
Hearing the tales of those who've failed and succeed
The monsters of fear and the dragons of self-doubt
cause me to sabotage my success and block
my efforts.
Action is my sword, confidence is my armor, and
my circle of friends is my shield.
These are my weapons to defeat these monsters and
slay these dragons.

(16)

Back to the Grind

My vacation has ended
My mind and body contented
All my aches left behind
Now back to the daily grind
(17)

Hunger

We'll stuff our mouths the first
chance we get,
even if we must nibble
on crumbs
But a hunger for our goal
we'll allow it to die unsatisfied.
(18)

Searching

Who am I
What is my goal
What should I write
Everyone writes of love
What makes me stand out
How am I different
Who am I
(19)

I am a Tree

I am a tree in a forest of millions of other trees.
our branches are separate, but our roots are tangled.
We may not know how or why but we're all bound
Whether you like me or not we are connected.
We all receive power from the same sun and
nourishment from the same rainfall. If we try to
poison others, we inevitably hurt ourselves.
We are known by the fruit we bear whether it is
actual fruit or leaves we help sustain nature.
We spread our seeds whether they are physical or
seeds of wisdom we share a part of ourselves with
those around us so we can all grow.
I am a tree in a forest of millions of other trees.

(20)

Mass Production

Mass production produces millions
of the same.
But handmade will give you pride
that can't be duplicated.
Mass production takes hours.
Handmade takes days or longer
Mass production produces millions
of the same.
But with handmade its imperfections
give it value.
Mass production produces millions
of the same.
But the defects of handmade makes
it one of a kind
(21)

Peace of mind

Creativity,
Plus, self-reflection and growth
From a quiet mind
(22)

My Hero

I AM MY HERO
I RESCUE MYSELF
I GET THE JOB DONE
I HAVE MY OWN BACK
(23)

To My Lovers

Thank you for the times that you've shared with me
your heart, your mind, and your body.
Thank you for the soft kisses, tender hugs, and
intimate nights.
Thank you for late-night text, morning coffee, jokes
and smiles.
Thank you for telling me your fears, your hopes
and intimacy
Thank you for making me a better companion, a
better man, and a better lover.

(24)

I Walked with Fear

Doubt pursued me and I fled
Criticism joined in and I ran faster
Motivation spoke up and I hid
Low self-esteem rose out of
the shadows, and I agreed
Encouragement whispered and
I stopped to listen
Pain sprang up and I hugged him
Hopelessness stood in front of me
and we became friends
Fear walked around the corner
I accepted his presence and walked with him.
Hope grabbed my hand and changed
my direction
(25)

Friends

I don't want to be your teacher
I want to be your friend
A teacher is looked up to as
knowledgeable
But friends learn from each other
I don't want to be your mentor
a mentor can help you grow
I want to be your friend so we can
grow together
I don't want to be your leader
I may not know which way to go
But as friends, we can find
the path together
(26)

Handling Extra

Do not waste extra money on
Liabilities invest instead
You can't save your way to wealth
But you must have a saving mentality
Invest your time and your money
into your mind.
(27)

Being Lucky

I watched Michael Jordan win six rings
and thought "he's really lucky"
When the Cubs won the World Series, I told
everyone that they were lucky.
When a coworker was promoted
to department manager
I said, "You're lucky."
I met a millionaire and asked him
"How did you get so lucky?"
He told me. "My luck began when
I became the best at one thing."
Everyone thinks it's luck when it's simply hard work
(28)

Hunt for Perfection

She dated a hundred men trying to find the one.
He jumped from one business idea to the next
searching for the one that would make him a
millionaire.
She spent months shuffling through career
options to decide which one pays the most.
He scoured social media
looking for the love of his life.
She looks for the nicest house
He hunts for the best car
Perfection doesn't exist
Yet everyone is disappointed
when they don't find it

(29)

The Positivity of Pain

Hardships, trials, and pain can change your perspective on life, the people around you, and yourself.

Accept struggles, don't hide or run from them.
They will teach you if you let them.
Pain can cause you to be afraid, or it can
fill you with courage.
Ask yourself what you can learn from this
Don't allow pain to break you, use it as a
source of strength and guidance.

(30)

AI Controversy

AI is a useful tool like a chisel or a scalpel.
They're only used to make your work easier.
If all you used was a scalpel all you could do is cut.
You need to know when to cut, when to clamp, when to stitch.
Using only one size chisel doesn't allow you to show the detail you envisioned.
Using AI to write the whole manuscript defeats the purpose and it weakens your creativity.
The purpose of a book is to connect your thoughts with the thoughts of the author.
To help you understand the world through the ideas of another person.
Experiencing the life of someone else whether they're real or fictional broadens your perspective of life.
An algorithm doesn't have a point of view about the world. It can't show you what it hasn't experienced
But it can help writers clearly express their ideas.

(31)

Heart Eyes

Lingering gaze
Passionate kiss
She blushes and
Sighs "I want you."
(32)

Your Name

Watching a movie.
The heroine had your name.
thoughts of you bounced around my mind
Every time someone mentioned your name
I remembered your face, your smile,
your laugh
I thought I was used to you not being around
I thought I couldn't be shaken by you anymore
But here is another rabbit hole, and
I'm ricocheting down
You echoed through my mind, your name just a whisper
The final leap over you that I must make
Just when I thought I cleared every barrier to
A life without you.

Ashes and Tears

Out of a need to cause trauma,
two sisters were attacked.
The city was struck in the heart,
loss of life and love.
The towers fell, they crumbled
the city was covered in
ashes and tears.
(34)

Be You

Don't be mad at anyone,
we are all living our lives
in the way that works best for us.
Liars believe they have a better
chance to get what they want by
being dishonest.
Honest people find that
being truthful works for them.
Decide what kind of person
you're going to be and be it.
(35)

v. A Limerick

There was a young man named Pete
He had very bad athlete's feet
He washed and he washed
The water he sloshed
And now they look like red meat

(36)

Self-Love

I accept myself as I am
I'm happy with myself
I appreciate myself
I know who I am
I believe in me
I trust myself
I love me

(37)

My Friend

Your eyes are not for my gaze
Your ears aren't for my praise
Your lips are not for my kisses.
Your body isn't for my touches.
You are not my woman or my lover
You're more for my growth than any other
(38)

Opposites

Yes, No
Kind, Bitter
Generous, Stingy
Wealth, Poverty
Riding, Walking
Talking, Silent
Good, Bad
(39)

I Don't Want to Live in Utopia

Utopia, a place without hardship or struggle may sound nice
but it will weaken my character and my mind
Utopia, a place without hardship or struggle may sound nice
but tough times have made me who I am
Utopia, a place without hardship or struggle may sound nice
but too much Pleasure and tenderness would soften my emotions
Utopia, a place without hardship or struggle may sound nice
but facing temptations and not giving in toughens my
character and emotions
Utopia, a place without hardship or struggle does sound nice
But then I wouldn't be me

(40)

Dance With Me

We sway as the music plays
Staring into each other's eyes
I sing the lyrics
when I add your name,
you blush
You pucker for a kiss
We stop dancing and
Fall in love
(41)

The Exit

"Are you stupid?" she screamed.
"That's the dumbest thing you've ever done."
I tried to make her happy but everything I did seemed to make it worse.
Flowers didn't work, singing failed, and poetry was garbage.
There was never any peace, every day, every action was never good enough.
Am I that much of a loser?
I endured it all until she felt her words weren't hitting hard enough and she switched to using her fist.
Then it was time to leave.

(42)

Not a Gentle Man

"Why don't you let the pregnant lady sit down, SIR?" A woman demanded of me.

"Why don't YOU let the lady sit down, ma'am?" I responded.

"Because I'm a woman."

"So, women don't have to let other women sit down?

It's only the man's obligation to make sure that a woman gets a seat?"

"Well, a gentleman would let the lady sit down."

"That's where you made your first mistake. I'm not a "gentle" man! But I am a kind man" I stand so the lady can sit.

(43)

Toxic

You love me then why do you lie?
You say that you can have sex with any guy
You love me then why do you stay out?
You say so you can date a different man to cause a bout.
You love me then why don't you hold my hand?
But you're happy to dance with any other man.
You say you love me then you say I'm jealous and act sad.
You give other men more attention, yet don't
understand why I'm mad.

(44)

Criminal

You should be arrested for
what you've done.
You should be tried, to the
fullest extent of the law.
They should lock you away
for your crime.
What you've done was
against our life
It was against our family
It was against our love
Sleeping with another is a
Relationship crime

(45)

Broken

What has been broken
can never be fully repaired
It can be mended but
it will never be the same
Whether it's a window, a toy, or trust
Things will never be the same

(46)

Your Rock

A man isn't strong because he has a hardened heart
but just the opposite. He's strong because his heart
is soft.
Not a soft character
A rock is strong for those who don't have his strength.
A rock is a support for those who can't stand on their own.
A rock says, I will hold you up until you find your own strength.
Put your worries on me and let me be your rock.

(47)

Helping

Income can only come
through helping others.
Every source of wealth
fulfills a need
It may seem heartless to say
but whether you like people or
not, helping is the answer to wealth
(48)

Where is the Me

Where is the me that you fell in love with?
Where did I go?
Why am I mean and jealous and self-centered?
What happened to the me that you fell in love with,
where did I go?
We laughed and loved and cried together
now I just wanna be left alone.
When did I leave where did I go,
where is the me that you use to love
where did I go?

(49)

To The Nerds

This is for us geeks, freaks, and nerds.
You're amazing, you're fascinating, you're epic.
Your creativity and your genius give the world new experiences a new piece of beauty.
Never strive to fit in. Don't let anyone put you in a box, in a room or a closet.
Knockdown the barricades, break down the walls, crash threw the door.
Show the world your uniqueness, your greatness, your strength, your wonderful self.
Stand strong, proud, and confident.
The geeks, the freaks, and the nerds, make the world beautiful.

(50)

Lost and Found

Lost:
Friendship
Trust
Love

—-

Found:
Confidence
Peace
Love
(51)

Press On or Give In

I can teach you what worked for me
I can show you every step of my way
You must learn your way
I can only be a guide
But your destination may be higher
or lower than mine
You have your own hills, trenches,
and battles to fight
You must decide if you will press on
or give in
Courage and confidence come
when you continue the fight,
but you must decide if you will
give in or press on.

(52)

Move On

You had your time to
fulfill your life's purpose
and to find true love
Let the younger generations
find their way
Don't allow jealousy to cause
you to hinder their pursuit
Look for the next step
in your journey and move on.
(53)

April's Showers

April walked up on August and June
Lying on the grass under the full moon
April thought herself a fool
How could the man she loved be so cruel
August jumped up and ran to her side
She pushed him away and began to chide
He attempted to reassure her that it was innocent
She refused to accept his lament
He tried to console her for hours but nothing he said
could stop April's showers.
(54)

A Royal Family

I am The King of my home!
My wife is not a servant or
a slave, but my Queen.
My son is not a page or
runner he is a Prince.
My daughter is not a maid or
helper she is a Princess.
We are a Royal Family
building our kingdom together

(55)

When Hope Fails

When hope fails
When hope is lost
When dreams have faded
You're left with a cold hard reality
A heavy heart and
nothing to look forward to
Hope is the reason to live
It is the goal to keep pressing on
Hope is the basis for thriving and
trying new fortes until you
encounter what works.
Though hope can periodically
appear to be a lost
keep going. it gives you the strength to fight on.
(56)

Working

The quality of your work
will determine how your
name is remembered
Whether you're cool and calm
or have a temper
Whether or not
you're the best in your field
Don't use anger as a shield
The quality of your work
depends on the
improvement of your skills.
(57)

Climbing

Concerned voices
will tell you to be careful.
You could get hurt.
That looks dangerous.
As you get higher, they'll say
you can't do it, you must stop.
You must go back.
Even your own voice
will tell you to give up.
To stop.
This is high enough.
You must climb past all those voices.
Until you reach the zenith
(58)

I Doubt My Words

I doubt my words and my skills
The more I learn the less I feel I know
I doubt my words and my skills
Am I real, am I clear, do my feelings show
I doubt my words and my skills
I'm looking, searching, hunting, for the right phrase
I doubt my words and my skills
Am I real, am I clear, do my feelings show

(59)

She Holds My Hand

She holds my hand when I need comfort
She holds my heart when I need love
She holds my mind when I need peace
She holds my body when I can't sleep
She holds my hand when I need a friend
She holds my heart when I need strength
She holds my mind when I need direction
She holds my body when I am cold
(60)

Winner

Be the winner,
be determined to succeed
Let someone else be the failure
let them decide they will lose
Be the one who knows
success is a mindset and
not luck
(61)

Solitaire Lessons

Most problems have a solution.
Some will be harder to find
but if you keep trying you
may find what works.
If you can't find an answer,
then you can confidently
move on knowing
you gave it your best effort.
(62)

Sleep

Why can't I sleep
What am I missing
what do I have to do
Why can't I sleep
Am I doing it to myself
Or are there real issues
I need to resolve.
Why can't I sleep
The alarm screams
I was asleep
(63)

Fatherless

Growing up fatherless a lot
of people will say they had less
Growing fatherless wasn't
a huge mess
Growing up fatherless hasn't
been the best
Growing up fatherless
means there's one less person
I need to try to impress
Growing up fatherless is nothing
new to process
Growing up fatherless is
knowledge I possess
(64)

Trying

Trying to make the right decision
Trying to take the right action
Trying to keep doubts from creeping in
Trying not to second-guess myself
Trying to ignore the negative
words of others
Trying to do my best
Trying is not doing
(65)

Limits

Mom told me that there
are two types of limits
The ones others put on us
and the ones we put on ourselves.
To reject the limits others,
attempt to put on us and
overcome the ones we place
on ourselves requires
the same solution... action.
(66)

YOLO

Yolanda rushed through every experience jumping
from lover to lover and not settling for love
Oscar's goal was wealth he didn't care who he hurt
or who hated him if he got paid.
Larry took his time with every experience he held on
to anger too long, he stayed in relationships he
should've let go of
Olivia was trapped in her own mind she wanted to
know herself but ended up lost in her own world
Living only once should be spent exploring yourself
And the world

I'm Sorry isn't Enough

My apology isn't enough
Numerous times you've told me how you felt
My apology wasn't enough
You told me how I treated you.
I am sorry didn't help
You let me into your life you shared yourself your
house your food and your body with me
I mistreated and took advantage of your gifts.
I'm sorry won't fix what I have done. it's too late to say "Thank you"
I'm sorry for being so late in my appreciation.
I am slow in growing up and maturing.
I see the error in my treatment of your generosity I'm
sorry isn't good enough. You're a precious gem.
And apologizing isn't enough.

(68)

You open yourself to me

You opened your mind, your home
and your body to me and I took advantage
You've shown me nothing but companionship
And compassion and I took advantage
I'm constantly looking for what I can
take but never what I can give
Now I open my heart to you so together
we can live
I've been so selfish and self-centered
that I've never let anyone in
Now I open my heart to you and invite you in
I open myself to you, my lover and my queen let me
have this chance to be your king
(69)

I Deserve

I deserve to be happy
I deserve to be successful
I deserve to be a millionaire
I deserve to be healthy and strong
But only if I put in the effort
(70)

The Positive Side of Negativity

Negativity can be a hindrance or a tool.
Negativity can come from others or yourself.
The words which may or may not be true can make
you doubt yourself, your skills, and your talent.
But it can also be a catalyst to push you forward.
When faced with negative thoughts don't try to
block them or shove them away, accept them as a
possibility then work so it doesn't happen.
You have an idea of what could happen
The Positive Side of Negativity
Go through the negative actions in
your mind learn from them
to lessen the chance of it happening in real life
Don't see negativity as an obstacle but as a tool.

(71)

Desire

After being in five relationships that ended badly, Ana gave up on dating altogether. She's been single for a year and a half and she's not looking for a boyfriend. When she meets her boss at her new job she feels an instant connection. He's mature, confident, handsome, and sexy as hell. The perfect man for her mom. But why can't she stop thinking about being with him? She doesn't like old men, but she wants this one

(72)

Sacrifices

For Success
- Family
- Sleep
- Happiness
- Vacations
- Validation
- Immediate desire
- Negative people

For love
- Wealth
- Partying
- Negative people
- Validation from others
- Selfishness

For a balanced life
- wealth
- Immediate desires
- Negative people
- Selfishness
- Validation
-

(73)

The Cycle Keeps Turning

Summer is the shortest season of the year, or does it
just seem that way because we look forward to it and
spend every day enjoying it
Autumn wakes our senses with brown, red, orange,
and yellow leaves, days ending early, as chilly
raindrops hit our faces.
Winter freezes our faces and fingers, our part of the
world is covered with ice and snow.
Spring brings us new life fresh flowers, green leaves,
and grass, birds chirping as they thaw eager minds
planking their summer fun.
The cycle keeps turning.

(74)

The First Day of Autumn

Its finally here
The rain, the cold, shorter days.
Its finally here
Stories of ghosts and goblins
and a pumpkin maze
Its finally here
Boots, sweaters, and coats
Its finally here
Sniffles, sneezes and sore throats
Its finally here
Holiday decorations being hung
Its finally here
The first days of Autumn has come

(75)

Poetic Journey

As I proceed on this poetic journey
Doubts, fear, and worry fill my mind.
Will I run out of what to say
will I forget how to write
I mustn't run from my anxiety
I must write about it
get it out, free my ideas and let them run wild
I must write out my fears
to liberate my mind from the cage of doubts.

(76)

You Can Make It Happen

God gave you the idea because
he knows that you can produce it,
It's your idea so make it happen.
God being there for you
is more than the world against you.
Even though you have doubts
he knows your capabilities
You can make it happen
(77)

Happiness Can Wait

He spent his days working nine-to-five, He would
sleep for four hours, then work from one to seven
When asked about his sleep he'd say,
"I'll sleep when I succeed."
His weekends were spent building his empire
He was asked if he was lonely,
didn't he want someone to love.
He said, "Love will come in time."
But he neglected time with his family and friends.
When asked if he was happy, he said
"Happiness can wait till next week."
But next week will only come after he succeeds

(78)

Support

A community having your back is empowering
Having a small circle builds confidence
A friend in your corner is better than being alone
Being alone is better than being surrounded
by negativity
Believing in yourself will get you to your goal
(79)

Decisions

Everyone has their opinion.
Everyone chooses how they're
going to treat others.
Action is a decision whether conscious
or unconscious,
You must decide if the negative
decisions of others
are going to affect your actions
(80)

Heart and Mind

You never know another person's heart or mind.
Friendliness, compassion, and interest can be faked.
You never know who wants to take advantage of you
or use you.
You never know who's with you for love or lust.
Who wants your money, your mind, your heart,
or your life
You never know a person's real thoughts,
but you can watch their actions
(81)

Not Your Mule

I was everyone's mule
the one called to move
and carry the heavy loads
But who was there for me?
I was a support, an ear, a warm hug
But I was left in the cold
I was everyone's free mule
I put my back
and muscles into every task,
But I had to pay strangers
for their back and muscles
I see pictures of the parties
and hanging out
I wasn't invited to
I sat at home alone
I'm tired of being the muscle,
the beast of burden,
the mule or was I a jackass.
(82)

A Wall

To protect your heart and sanity
Put up stop signs and maybe a barricade
but not a wall.
Boundaries are the warning signs
that say proceed with caution
Walls block everything, not just hurt, but also love.
Be the overseer until you must be the warrior
Give warnings but don't tolerate disrespect
A wall does keep out enemies, but also friends
(83)

A Million Tears

We shared a thousand laughs and shed a million tears
We celebrated the start of every year and reminisced
about our foolishness and the lessons, we learned.
You were my window to the world now you're only
a memory of the days and love we've shared.
We shared a thousand laughs now I shed a million tears.
(84)

Flowers on the Path

While striving to make your fortune
Enjoy the success you have
While reaching for the distant stars
Take time to appreciate what is near
While running to achieve that goal
Take time to walk with those cheering you on
While grinding on the road to be a millionaire
Enjoy the smell of the flowers on the path
(85)

Nature's Cruelest Crime

I had an insatiable desire
that women would admire
Time slowly took my strength,
but my appetite remained
Satisfying this hunger
became tougher over time
My decline is
nature's cruelest crime
Tried exercise, pills, and diet but
nature is stronger than my desire.
(86)

Shutters Latched

Windows locked, shutters latched, blinds closed,
and curtains drawn never to be opened again.
Hide the sunrise, noonday sun, setting sun
I don't want to see the romance again
Morning hugs, afternoon kisses,
and nighttime love won't be anymore
Hourly conversation, daily singing, weekly laughing
missing you since you walked away.
Now I sit alone in my room
Windows locked, shutters latched, blinds closed,
and curtains drawn never to be opened again.
(87)

Trauma

We voluntarily traumatize, ourselves
and call it entertainment.
Watching violent, bloody, and gory
movies.
Movie trauma only lasts for an hour
and ends with hope or victory
Real-life trauma can last
for weeks, or months,
affecting us for the rest of our lives
and not always ending in victory.
(88)

Luck or Skill

I wanted to be lucky.
I wanted to live by chance
I thought luck
would bring me the job,
the woman, and the wealth
I desired.
I always thought fate
Would bring good things to me.
But after many knockdowns and
rejections, I see the only way to get
everything I wanted is by activity
by skills and talent.
Success comes from skill
and a little luck
(89)

A Planned Life

A life without direction ends in misery.
A life without a plan doesn't go anywhere
A life without an agenda winds up in poverty
A life without a goal doesn't have any rewards
A life without purpose is empty
A life without ambition falls into despair
A life without hope ends in sorrow
A life without love ends in loneliness

(90)

Trashy Tracey

Trashy Tracey tried to attack my brain.
Blending brackish verbs binding bitter words
she belittled my world.
Whirling wasteful witticisms around my mind
Muttering meaningless phrases made me agitated
Approaching her I articulated awareness of her rage
Retracking, she relented and repented
The wrong was righted she walked away delighted.

(91)

Prison Break

I'm a prisoner of his words, endless stories of people
I don't know, who are doing things I don't care about.
My desk is my cell, his stories my prison bars
holding me captive, no way to escape.
I formulate a jailbreak, the toilet my refuge. I tell the
warden with his worrisome words, that I need to
relieve myself.
He says, okay, the cell collapses, I walk away.
I need a better plan, to avoid being a jailbird, held by
his multitude of words.

(92)

Babbling Brooke

Babbling Brooke, like an endless river
running over stones her voice rattles on and on
Talkative Trish, stops at my desk
and buzzes on about her husband and kids
she is as annoying as a horde of cicadas
Gossiping Greg, is like a sponge
he sucks up garbage about everyone's life
and then wrings it out on anyone he can get to listen
Ranting Rita, spreads misery like chunky peanut butter
on bread
her stories must be worse than anyone else's
making her spread it thicker and thicker until
even she doesn't know when it's too much

(93)

Idle Hands

Lifeless mounds of flesh, my hands lay on the desk
waiting for the energy to write.
Thoughts rise slowly like a swallowtail butterfly
lifting off a branch.
Rising, hovering, drifting into the ether
Weighed down by thoughts of the work needed
my hands don't move to the keyboard
My mind is lazy won't put in the effort to create
my hands lay on the desk waiting
for the words to write.

(94)

Wasting Rhymes

What should I write, what should I say
My words stray, am I any good or am I
Just wasting my words
I don't seek the approval of others,
but I wonder what they think
Are my skills outdated am I just wasting their time
I feel untalented, and unskilled I study, I write, I learn
but it never feels good enough like I'm wasting
rhymes

(95)

Words

Words are fleeting I don't know what to say.
Using them to communicate to express how I feel
Whether verbal or written I work to be understood
My words are holding me back
I need them to learn and to grow
Friendly and polite or harsh and mean
Using their sound and my tone to
express my thoughts.
Words are my friends

(96)

Heart Attack

My wife, my lover, my best friend
was having a heart attack.
She needed an ambulance, ASAP, I placed the
emergency call and told them of the situation.
I was assured someone was on the way.
"How're you doing, someone is coming," I said,
comforting her. "Hold on my love."
The doorbell rang, I ran and opened the door,
the Paramedics with their gurney rushed to her side
"How're you feeling, do you have tightness in your
chest?"
A few questions while they performed a few tests,
they assisted her on the gurney.
I locked up as we all left,
we arrived at the hospital just in time.
Her heart continues to beat,
The attack on her heart abated.

(97)

Almost Friday

Monday morning, preparing for another day of labor
to greet the customers and help them solve their issues
it's almost Friday only four more days
Tuesday morning, same time and thing as yesterday
a repeat of the weeks and months before it's almost
Friday three more days
Wednesday already, Friday is almost here only two
days left it's all downhill from here
Thursday, or as I like to call it Friday Eve, one more
day and my weekend can begin
It's Friday, the day has finally come. I keep my mind
busy, so I don't watch the clock.
The day is finally over two off days and the cycle
starts again.

(98)

Just a Taste

I want a taste of your soft
and pretty lips,
a nibble on your sensitive neck
Little kisses across your chest
Butterfly kisses on your belly
To your hips and your sweet thighs
your calves, feet, and toes
then to your treasure-trove
I want just a taste,
I want to savor every inch.
(99)

Tats

With ink pens, erasers,
an ink gun we decorate our skin
Animals, names, abstract

(100)

Tears

Why
Why do I cry
Tears trickle
from my eyes
I don't know why
I cry
Sorrowful tears
A sadness deep
Inside
Why
Why do I cry
(101)

Selected

Scientists tell us
the odds of a specific person
being born is 1 in 400 quadrillion.
I don't think we are random
I think we were selected
each of us were chosen
I don't think we were
1 out of 400 quadrillion.
I think we are
THE 1 out of 400 quadrillion.
(102)

Come to Me

Come to me she whispered in my ear
come to me, darling let me hold you near
Come to me, my lover, she blushed at me
come to me, my dear, let me sit on your knee
Come to me, sweetheart, I want to cuddle
Come to me, my man, let's make a sweaty puddle
Come to me, my sweet honeybee
Come to me, yes, yes, yes, my King, she said,
come inside me

(103)

Dancing on the Edge

Precariously on the precipice
Between delight and danger
Whirling and twirling to see
which way will win
Playing and grinning
Thinking life is a game
Slipping and sliding life
won't be the same
Fall into danger,
end up as vapor
Tumbling into delight
won't be much better
(104)

Backseat

It's easy to give directions from the passenger seat
Sitting in the driver's seat is when life changes
Talking without experience is simple
Doing the work changes the conversation
Sitting on the sideline it's easy to criticize
Running the race changes the perspective
It's easy to point out what's wrong from the backseat
But from the front you can see clearly

(105)

The Rescue

The scream of the smoke detector broke the night's
Silence, and Ashley's sleep. In a panic, she jumped from
the bed and ran into the smoke-filled living room wearing
her pajamas.
"What's burning?" she thought. She coughed, her lungs
filled with the harsh fog and collapsed.
Before she blacked out two firemen burst into the apartment, smoke billowing in behind them.
A blanket wrapped around her shoulders,
she was lifted and carried to the hall, down the stairs,
and into the fresh night air.
"Is anyone else in there, Miss?"
"No. what happened?"
"We're investigating."
Her nose filled with the aroma of smoke, ash,
and singed hair, the cologne, all firefighters wear.
It was a cool summer night but, her adrenaline, and the
arms of the man who just saved her life kept her warm.

(106)

A Kind Young Man

Out of high school,
straight into boot camp.
Arms got stronger, legs faster,
climbed the stairway to heaven,
jumped through the hell hole,
slid down the slide of life.
Learned to shoot,
we marched everywhere,
We marched day and night.
Trained how to fight, taught
military history and how
to be confident and proud
Raised to be friendly and kind,
trained to take a life,
how to take a man down
went from being a kind young man
to being a government trained killer.
(107)

Cheating

“So much more satisfying than my husband,” Sharon said, slipping on her panties.

"Then leave him and move in with me."

"He pays for our hookups, and he has no idea." squeezing her double-Ds in her bra."

"Being with me is better than building your marriage bond?"

I took my phone to the washroom and sent a message.

"With you and him I have a perfect man." She laughed, "A man, with lots of money and a man, with lots of “manhood."” She grinned devilishly scanning down my body.

I tossed my phone on the bed.

"You don't feel terrible?" I asked, putting on my pants, my phone buzzed.

"Why should I? I'm sure he's doing the same. Why do you care about him anyway?" She had on her blouse and skirt and sat in a seat to slip on her shoes.

"Just being selfish, wondering, if you were my wife."

"Keep satisfying me. you won't have anything to worry about."

"But you will."

"What?"

I walked to the door.

One knock

Before she inquired who was there her husband entered

(108)

Living

I write,
I sing,
I play,
I dance.
I love,
I live,
I date,
I romance.
(109)

Dawn

The sun rises over the Eastern horizon.
Dawn is sitting at the lake absorbing
The first sunrays shining on her face.
A cool breeze blowing away
the arguments of last night.
Something shifted in her mind.
She couldn't explain it if she tried
Her spirit was touched by
the calmness of the morning.
A blissfulness arose in her heart.

She realized the shallowness of the fight with her husband, how pointless it all seemed now.

They could settle this together.

(110)

The Clock

Tick, tock, tick, tock
The clock doesn't stop
It ticks for the woman
But his clock is ticking too
She won't be able to bring
someone new into the world
He won't be able to rise for
the situation,
Their days of reproducing
Have come to an end
Pills and other methods can
keep the pleasure going
but they are freed from childbearing
(111)

Talent and Skill

Talent - the natural ability to see how things
fit.
Skill - hours and hours of improving technique
Together you'll be impossible to beat
(112)

Strings

I didn't know our connection had strings
Our affiliation depended on
how useful I was to you
You were the manipulator,
the con artist trying to obtain all you can,
you were never my friend and
now our association ends.
(113)

The Heartbreak Kid

Steve and Sarah, six years together.
Sarah was a great girlfriend, she was supportive, she
would turn down other guys, she only wanted him.
Steve couldn't sit still he wanted the next woman,
the next thrill.
Steve was getting uptight it was time for him to take
flight
He would criticize everything Sarah tried.
He tried to break her heart like he'd done with other
women in the past.
She saw his scheme and knew it wasn't worth the
trouble and left him to reap his karma.

(114)

Writing

Morpheus said it best,
"Some rules can be bent, others, can be broken."
The wisdom is knowing one from the other
and when to capitalize.
Writing is a living breathing entity
it can be killed with too many pretty words
or with too few.
If nurtured just right, it can bloom

(115)

Negative Thoughts

I remember my mistakes, mistreatments,
and bad things that I've done.
I try to tell myself "Oh well, forget it, it's gone."
But it doesn't go away, it comes to my mind
over, and over again.
I've learned to accept the negative things
that I've said and done.
To help myself see the situation
and what can I learn.
I write the incidents and lessons
in my journal and often review them,
so they don't reoccur.

(116)

Chillin'

"Aren't you tired from cleaning windows all day?
Don't you wanna break, don't you wanna chill?"
"I am Chilling. This isn't work, this is how I break."
"That's too much for me."
"Your eight-hour workday is occasionally interrupted
by a break. Whereas my eight-hour break is
occasionally interrupted by mealtime.
I enjoy doing this so it's not like work.
It isn't fun but it isn't work."

(117)

Simp

Too friendly
Too sweet
Too kind
Too helpful
Too caring
Too agreeable
Too nice
(118)

Bittersweet Kisses

Lips, so soft on mine,
making my heart race
Pulling you into
a tighter embrace,
your beautiful perfume
and the gentle touch of your lips
draws me in it is a state of Zen.
But your words don't make
me feel the same
they are harsh to my heart.
The sound breaks me down
bringing my spirit low
the words wound and are so bitter
How can the lips that bring so much
pleasure says words that break my heart.
(119)

Communication

Not speaking
the same tongue,
we can't communicate
We feel left out
of the conversation,
especially with our mate
To build our kinship we must
take the time, we must apply
the effort to comprehend
(120)

Stone and Sky

We live our lives between
the stone and the sky.
Stone being struggle
and sky being peace of mind.
We Spend too much
of our time trying to avoid
the stones
in constant pursuit of the sky.
But if we accept the stones
as part of everyday life,
we will reach the sky.
(121)

Message in a Bottle

I Set sail on the ocean of life, my ship was thrashed,
and smashed by winds and tempest.
I held on to the raft that was left of my ship
and landed on a sandy shore
Stranded on an island with no shelter
and nowhere to hide.
While scavenging I found a glass bottle
with faded paper inside.
Curiosity got the better of me, I smashed it into a rock.
Gently I unfolded it. "Welcome to the land of love.
The storms on the ocean of life have brought you
To this shore. You have the option to stay or leave, life won't be easy, but in the end, you will be satisfied.
If you want to go back to the ocean
there's a boat on the other side of the island."
I stayed.

(122)

Smoke and Ash

"FIRE!" A voice screamed
"Where are you?" I responded
"FIRE!"
"Where?"
"Inside the smoke, covered in ash."
After a few seconds I saw the was smoldering ash.
Cautiously I pushed it aside, till I felt a tiny lump.
A bright red bird moved, shifted, and looked up at me.
Shaking its body, his wings spread out. I placed him
on the ground as he slowly grew larger.
He grew to my height and spoke.
"I am you. The fire that ignited in your heart,
has caused me to grow. Burning off the old beliefs,
and ideas giving birth, to a new level of you. Now let's fly."
I spread my fiery wings and floated into the sky.
With one flap I was on a mission, for the next peak.

(123)

Full of Love

I'm so full of..." LOVE," right now.
I'm trying to hold it in, I must release it.
I'd like to share it with you,
I don't know how long I can hold out.
This love is building up inside me.
I miss the weight of your body on top of me,
as you rock and squeeze me.
I miss the song you sing when your love builds
and releases on me.
I miss how you'd rock and coax my love
from me and allow it to fill you.
I miss how we'd hug and cuddle
in the afterglow of sharing our love.

(124)

Strangers on a Train

Riding the train home one night, I had the car to myself.
I busied myself on social media, I didn't notice
the cute woman wearing a tight, low-cut pink blouse,
revealing her D cleavage, and the obvious nipple imprint.
Her short summer skirt flared as she sat across from me.
We stared into each other's eyes, she blushed, inch by
inch she raised her skirt, and opened her legs revealing her
thighs until she exposed her naked and smooth honeypot.
Standing, she put one foot on the empty seat next to me,
and stretched out her hand, I put my hand in hers,
she guided my hand to her wetness,
she began breathing heavily as I played with her,
she moaned when I slipped two fingers inside,
and her fluids ran down my arm.
Her foot slipped to the floor; we kissed.
She wrapped her arms around my neck and moaned
loudly in my ear as she came.
"Thank you, sir. I needed that. Now let's go home.
I want you to make me cum again in our bed."
My wife and I hugged and kissed, until we got to our stop.

(125)

Distractions

When you're reaching for your goal, and you're easily
Distracted, either you're losing interest, or you need
a break.
Why are you losing interest? Is it not as exciting
as it used to be?
You need to reevaluate, if you're willing
to put in the months or years it may take
to realistically reach your goal.
If you need a break, then take it.
Taking a day or at most a week off is recommended,
it gives your mind and body a rest period and you can
come back energized and with new ideas.
Going after your goal is your responsibility
You can hire people to help you, but the final
accountability falls on your shoulders.

(126)

Kiss Me

"Kiss me." I demanded her
"No... Okay, just one. Muah."
"That was..."
"One more. Muah."
"I'm gonna kiss you back."
"I dare you!"
"Challenge accepted."
"I'm gonna tell my brother."
"Why, he already knows."
"He knows what, that we kissed?"
"That I've been wanting to kiss you."
"But does he know
that I want to kiss you too?"
"He does now. He's right behind you."
(127)

Born Again

Friend: Do you believe in reincarnation?
Me: Yes. Because my carnations grow back every year.
Friend: I mean do you believe that we come back here to live again.
Me: Why would anybody wanna come back here?
Once is enough for me.
Friend: Wouldn't you want to come back and fix your
mistakes?
Me: if I did come back, it would be as a different
person so the mistakes, I made in this life would
never get fixed.

(128)

Amber

Going to work, a train pulls into
the Berwyn station, doors slide open.
Standing room only. The train sways down the track
as I scan the crowd looking for a familiar face.
There she is two seats down. She looks up.
We smile and nod at each other.
At Belmont, the girl next to her Stands up.
I move toward it, but a senior beats me.
Doors close.
I'm jolted backwards moving me farther away.
I summoned my courage to speak to her, but the train
wasn't going to make it simple.
Six stops later she stands hands me a folded paper
and exits.
Her name, and number.
I smile.

(129)

Mutations

Growth, change, development.
Sometimes improvements, sometimes
regression, but definitely different.
People run from stressed environments
but that is where growth happens
time and patience bring mutations
Some physical, some mental, or
emotional development.
But we all mutate

(130)

Love is a Four-Letter Word

The word "Love"
is tossed around like children playing hot potato
it has almost lost its true meaning
compassion, help, kindness.
People act like it needs to be handled with kid gloves,
like it's fragile, and could break
Love is strong and tough, if given the chance,
it can handle many hard situations
Love is not only an emotion, but also an action.
Not a sexual act, but, expressed through
kindness, friendliness, and compassion.
Love is a small word, but its effects are powerful.

(131)

Laughter

I love to laugh
I love making others laugh
I've tried my hand at humor.
But my jokes come off
As boring and flat
I must study the rhythm
And the rhyme
And know when the line has
been punched.
(132)

A Grande Blonde

"Good morning, sir, what can I get started for you?"
"Morning, I want a medium-height blonde,
that gives sweet kisses
and who has an extra inner strength
that will help me get through my day."
"I'm sorry. What?"
"I want a Grande blonde with a shot of Expresso
with sugar and cream. Thanks."
"Ooookay."

(133)

I shouldn't Hide

I'm told that I should hide for a season then show up and surprise the world.
I think the reason I'm told to hide is to stay away from the negative voices.
But I feel in order to grow I need
to fail in front of a group of haters.
Yes, it'll be hard, but it builds strength of character.
If I hide and learn and write, then step out when I'm ready, no one will know who I am. But if I write in the face of my haters then I'll build courage and mental fortitude.

(134)

Wounds

I hurt myself more than anyone else could
My words have broken my heart
more than anyone else's words could
I lied to myself more than anyone else has
I deceived myself more than anyone else has
I've harmed myself more than anyone else did
I've made myself cry more than anyone else did
I've believed in myself more than anyone else has
I've trusted myself more than anyone else has
I've encouraged myself more than anyone else did
I've had my own back more than anyone else did

(135)

Attention

Attention to, detail
Patience in the process
Learning from every error
Knowing that slow growth
brings sustainable success
Each improvement
Doubles confidence and knowledge
Success starts with attention
(136)

Alpha

Alpha - a leader, not boss
Alpha - shows the way
Alpha - discovers and
encourages strengths
Alpha - instructs on boosting
weaknesses
Alpha - teaches independence
(137)

Apathy

Apathy causes failure
working on your weaknesses
Builds strength and skills
(138)

Being Bold

I'm pulled into
Confrontations I tried to avoid
I'm drawn into defending my stance.
I doubt my skills in getting my point across
I think I'll look like a fool
I must clearly understand
my idea
and boldness will come
(139)

Bungalow

Our bungalow, our vacation home
Near the ocean, a beautiful place to roam
A place to explore nature and each other.
Resting under the palm trees,
Strolling along the sandy shore
A hug, a kiss, a race into the rising tide
Back to our bungalow, our vacation home
A little slice of happiness, we call our own
(140)

Beautiful Woman

Steve walks into work and sees Rita at the water cooler.
"Rita," he says when he approaches the cooler.
Looking up, her smile exposes her joy,
Her dark eyes shine, revealing her love
She pushed her hair behind her ear, bearing her neck
"Good morning," she timidly speaks,
trying to hide her desire
He lifts her chin, leans forward,
and kisses her cheek.
"Good morning, my beautiful woman."
"Am I, your woman?"
"No. You're my, BEAUTIFUL, woman"
Her smile broadens, cheeks reddening,
She turns to skip away.
Steve grabs her hand. "Where are you going?"
"Nowhere, sir." She turns to his embrace.

(141)

Chicago

A wide field of wild onions
Home of the Potawatomi
a trading post
a home
a town
a city
A close community
A neighborhood
A home
Friends
Family
History
(142)

Comfort Zone

A place in your mind
A place of ease and little stress
A place we're encouraged
To not do our best
The comfort zone is a place to hide
It's a place where our fears reside
A place we seek a pat on the back
Where we lose track of years
Where we dream and fantasize
Where we never plan
and our dreams are not realized
We must escape our comfort zones
We must plan
and act before
we rest,
underneath a tombstone
(143)

Corona

A corona is a circle of light
around a luminous object.
We are to be
the circle of light of the world
Our inner glow of friendship,
kindness, and compassion
God is the luminous object inside us,
and we are his
Corona shining in the world
(144)

Distance

Jake's promotion
took him a thousand miles away.
Sharon was in his
thought's night and day
He called her before work and after,
he told her jokes
just to hear her laughter
Making time to come together
was getting harder
She was scared to leave
the life she knew
She grieved being without him
The distance between them
became too much to handle
Fear was her hindrance
to being with, the man she loved
But was her fear the distance,
or giving in to true love
(145)

Delusional

Am I delusional to believe I can accomplish this feat
or am I just doubting my ability?
The goal is obtainable, and I'm the one who can achieve it.
It won't be easy, but I won't give up.
Anyone else's doubt holds no clout.
My poems may not be the best,
but my words won't be lost in the chasm of time
They may be corny and meaningless to some
but I'm doing my best in pursuing my dream.
I might be delusional but there are worse delusions to pursue.

(146)

Diamond in the Rough

Every diamond
no matter how small
has the potential to catch everyone's eye
It's not easy to notice a diamond
or to tell its true quality until
it is cut, shaped, and smoothed
The facets must be perfect for that gem
and deeply polished to reveal
its distinct glimmer within

(147)

Everlast

We grinned at one another and, soon we held hands
We hugged each other, and the kissing began
We had a fight and, we each went our own way
While living our lives we met once again
We sat and talked and, kissed once more
We missed one another and,
decided to give it a second chance
This time we were better,
we were more mature
This time we talked
instead of fought

(148)

Expressing Love

When I was young, expressing love
and being romantic was the norm.
Most of our songs
were to win her heart
to make her feel special
that she was the only one.
Buying a girl flowers and, giving her gifts would win
her heart
Now before she'll go on a date, you must ignore her
to make her chase you
You must push her away, to make her stay.

If you buy her flowers or tell her she's cute, she'll think you're weak and not worth her time.

Women used to love a man who could
sing and dance but now, he doesn't stand a chance.
Women used to complain that their man wasn't
Home, now they complain when he is home.

(149)

Echo

The words and pictures
that bounce around in your
mind make you, you
What rebounds off the walls
of your thoughts must
change in order to have
the life of your dreams
Changing the echo in your mind
combined with action and daily grind
Echoing the pictures and emotions
of your goal will reinforce your words,
and actions, and the result.
(150)

Fresh Air

I inhale deeply, taking in
the sweetness of the freshly mowed grass,
and lilacs planted by the neighbor
a hint of rain from last night's shower.
Nature scrubbed the air clean
from car exhaust, cigarette smoke, and trash.
The fresh air soothes my senses
and clears my mind.
For right now my worries are gone
and my head is clear.
(151)

Fine Wine

Your character is like fine wine
Smooth Courage in handling difficult people,
Sweet Character and grace in tough situations,
Balanced Attention to detail in pursuit of dreams,
Earthy Wisdom in seeking and using knowledge,
A subtle crisp kindness,
Refreshing readiness and willingness to assist,
A velvety wine that adds spice to my life.

(152)

Failing

Excuses give you a reason to give up.
Excuses give you a reason to not apply yourself.
Excuses makes you see the clouds instead of the lining
Excuses you find the struggle to every success
Excuses give you a motive to doubt
Excuses make you see failure as a reason to stop

(153)

Guided Resurrection

When I woke up this morning, I heard a whisper.
"Your mind is clouded, and darkness covers
your thoughts, you need a resurrection of your mind.
You may think that happiness and love are dead but I'm
here to resurrect it if you allow me to be your guide."
"Guide me," I said out loud. "Please show me the way."
"Remember running, playing, laughing, and the fun
you had with your family?
Think of your first crush, do you remember that feeling?
Don't worry about remembering her name,
what's important is the emotion.
That was love, before manly thoughts started to infiltrate.
Think about the pets you raised and loved, they only had
companionship to offer, which you gladly accepted.
Remember how giving to those in need filled your heart?
The joy of compassion is another form of love."
Water filled my eyes and trickled down my cheeks,
empathy overflowed my heart.
My resurrection was beginning

(154)

Grandiose

To people near you, you may seem feeble
your dreams may seem more than you can handle
More complicated than necessary, imposing, or over-exaggerated.
because it's not their dream
They think that it's just a scheme
They expect you to fail and are waiting to say
that your dreams seem too ambitious for you.
As grandiose as it may seem, continue to press
towards your dream.

(155)

Gumption

Having an easy life will make you weak.
Only resistance can build strength.
Guarding yourself from bad situations will break you
Some obstacles can't be avoided
but they can be overcome, either by
climbing over, digging under, going around,
or punching threw.
Don't let obstacles stop you. You might have to
pause while you plan your next move but push
through.

(156)

Happy Birthday

I'm sending you this birthday wish
May your day bring you laughter and bliss
Another year to be alive
another chance to strive for your slice of life
I hope joy, peace, and happiness
fill your following year
may laughter and love keep you smiling
from ear to ear
(158)

Honey Buns

The overhead doorbell rang when I entered the bakery,
the aroma of freshly baked bread pulling me to the counter.
"I'll be right there," the young woman announced.
Her back was to me, her long hair coiled
into a beehive with a net covering.
Her apron was cinched on her small waist.
I wondered how someone could work in a bakery
and have such a nice figure. If I worked here,
I'd weigh a ton.
My eyes drifted to the buns, I couldn't look away.
So full and round I wanted to hold them in my hands
They looked so soft and spongy I wanted to squeeze
each one
Lustrous and sweet looking, my mouth watered
I was eager to take a bite
"Nice buns," I exclaim
The sales lady giggled and shyly turned and faced me
"You like what you see?"
"Yes, they look so delicious, let me have three."
She looked confused and then disappointed when she
realized I meant the buns in the case.

(159)

Hoggish

"Linda, will you stop."
"Stop what Jake?"
"Stop acting like you're into me."
"I am. Why wouldn't I be, you're handsome, smart, funny?"
"We've worked together for eight years, and you've never shown interest before."
"Well, I'm interested now."
"But I'm seeing someone else."
"She's not right for you."
"You just got married, so you're not right for me either.
After you walk down the aisle, and I move on you decide
you want to be with me!? That sounds greedy."
"Greedy, what do you mean?"
"You only want me when someone else does,
you want your admirer back. Stop being hoggish
and let me move on."

(160)

Ink

In grammar school, we used ink pens
to write on ourselves and pretend they were tattoos.
We bought temporary tattoos from the gumball machine
and showed them off like they were real
In high school, we used pencil erasers to erase our skin
making more permanent marks on ourselves,
I still have the "T" I scraped into my skin
After graduating from Boot Camp,
I and a few fellow Marines went to a tattoo parlor
and had our skins decorated with real needles and ink. Not a gentle process
but a cool symbol of being a badass.

(161)

Is Love Ancient

Is love an ancient ideal from ancient times or...
Is it the standard for today
Is love an ancient thought from ancient times or...
Is it thought about today
Is love an ancient action from ancient times or...
Is it performed today
Is love an ancient thing from ancient times or...
Is it an object that is used today
Is love an ancient emotion from ancient times or...
Is it in people's hearts today
Is love an ancient word from ancient times or...
Is its meaning still alive in the world today
If love is an ancient dream from ancient times, can we make it relevant today

(162)

Ignoring your disapproving eyes

You roll your eyes when I speak of my goals
You look to the sky when I talk of the actions I took
You give me the side-eye when I speak of the things I try
You buck your eyes when I talk of my good luck
So much disbelief and disapproval are expressed in your eyes, but I ignore it all and continue to strive

(163)

Jellyfish

Her moves are fluid like the waves of the ocean
Her limbs are like ripples each making its presence obvious
Her motions pulled him in
They spin like two weather systems fighting for dominance
He directs her like the captain of a ship
They handle the demands of their movements together as one body
Their dance becomes an emotion
The emotion is love

(164)

Judgment

Sixty-six days to change a habit, ninety days to change our mindset.
Our habits are your actions, our mindset is knowing why
you're doing it
Scarcity, our first reason to change mindset.
Abundance, is our new mindset
Our habits are for us, our mindset is for the world.

(165)

Jack

For Jack, the worst things about being in a war
were the dreams he had when you came home.
Trying not to remember the faces of the men
he's killed and, trying not to remember
the lifeless faces of his fellow Marines.
The only thing that could wash away his thoughts
was alcohol.
He always stayed past the last call.
It was never easy for Jack to cope.
The thoughts would return two, three, maybe
four times a day, he never found any hope.
Whenever he found a reason to laugh or smile
he would think how the men that he killed and
his friends would never laugh again.
Even if the government said they were the
"enemy" didn't they deserve a chance
to laugh and love?

(166)

Kissing Game

I watch your perfectly shaped lips as
our faces slowly come together.
Pausing an inch from each other
we tease and tempt one another.
Peppermint wafts from your smiling mouth
Our closeness tests our weakness
who will be the first to surrender
Your pupils dilate as our souls unite
Electricity shoots through my body
when you press your soft breast into my chest
I pucker my lips to tempt you
You succumb, lean in and our lips finally touch.
We embrace as our desires rise
I caress you as our inhibitions fade
and our craving increases,
we allow ourselves to give in to our urges.

(167)

Knack

I remember when Tupac first came on the scene.
Everyone was praising him and talking about his rap talent
One of my ex-wife's nephews got pissed and said that he
was a better rapper than Tupac. He was so angry at Pac's
success.
But the nephew didn't participate in talent shows or
competitions. He didn't put himself out there to get
recognized. He hated a man who had more
courage to pursue his dreams.

(168)

Keys to the Throne

Random acts of love
Seeing a need and helping
Are keys to the throne

(169)

Lady in Lavender

She hated the word purple it is now such a common word
lilac, mauve, periwinkle, plum.
These colors were a little better,
but none seemed to fit her taste
She wanted something different something that would
make her stand out.
Lavender was softer, the dress seemed a bit more
seductive
The color highlighted her eyes, and the design emphasized
the effort she put in at the gym
She wanted Patrick to admire her, the way she thought
of him all these years.
She wanted to be his lady in lavender

(170)

Loves Last Call

She called me to her side
we walked, talked, laughed, and lied
She whispered that she loved me, but I knew it wasn't true
she only wanted what I could do
She wanted me to hold her hand
and to tell her that I loved her too
I was too afraid of love and the hurt that it can cause
I was too afraid to live alone, I didn't want to be isolated
She didn't want to waste her life
waiting for a love that
may never come so she walked away
in search of a love that would stay

(171)

Leaves of Gold

Golden leaves at sunset, a chilling breeze
Golden leaves at sunset, a rustle of leaves
Golden leaves a sunset, walking hand in hand
Golden leaves at sunset, we didn't have a plan
Golden leaves at sunset, we sat on a bench
Golden leaves at sunset, we made a pledge
Golden leaves at sunset, the time for marriage is now
Golden leaves at sunset, we walked down the aisle
Golden leaves at sunset, we made our vow

(172)

Magic

Despite all the doubts about magic, I know magic is real
Magic is the smile I get from the thought of your face
Magic is the butterflies I get when I hold your hand
Magic is my racing heart when I kiss your lips
Magic is the warmth I feel when you say my name
Magic is the confidence I feel when you appreciate my efforts
Magic is the joy I have when you laugh at my jokes
Magic is the days and nights we spent together
Magic is you and I in love

(173)

Move On

You think ignoring her will make her miss you.
But you're doing exactly what she wants you to do.
You think she'll come running
to see why you're not paying attention to her.
But she's happy that you left her alone, isn't that clear
Now you wonder what you should do.
Move on with your life, find someone else
to give your time and attention
Don't pretend to move on thinking it will bring her back.
Move on and get your life on track

(174)

Messy

"Why do you wanna date me?" Susan asked
"What do you mean?"
"You know what I mean. Do you just wanna sleep with me,
or do you want to make my life better?"
"That's selfish of you. Do I want to make your life better."
"That's what couples are supposed to do, improve each
other's lives. I'm willing to help you accomplish your
dreams are you willing to put in the effort to help me
achieve mine?"
"Huh."
"That's what I thought. You just want sex. Goodbye."

(175)

Night Work

Working my brain through the night
Searching for the right expressions
Stretching my vocabulary, growing my word count
Building on what I know and pushing away sleep
The night work is part of the process
Sleep doesn't matter, only the work is important,
where talent leaves off skills must arise.
The night work must continue
to break through the wall of talent

(176)

Neptune

Deep in the dark and cold,
not hiding just waiting for the spark
The jolt of adoration the tingle of growth
Sitting in the depths with the power to fulfill dreams
Like Neptune in the ocean's depths, Christ is waiting
He wants to take control of the ocean of your ambitions
He wants to direct the actions as your ideas flood your senses
Give him a flicker of faith and he will guide the waves

(177)

November Nights

A heater and blankets keep away the November night's chill
But it's still a poor substitute for the void that I feel
The scent of your body the caress of your hand
Your absence makes my November nights hard
The dark comes early, and the nights are long
I miss your sweet song,
The November nights have a deep chill
Yes, Jill I need to hold you in my arms
You are the balm to these cold November nights.

(178)

Others

You were trying to be my friend
and I was trying to befriend
others.
You looked up to me and I was
looking up to others
You wanted my help, and I was
trying to get help from others
You wanted my advice, and I was
trying to advise others
You wanted to be around me
and I was trying to get around others
I put others ahead of our
friendship and realized too late
that I lost you to them
I put my admiration for others
ahead of you and you started
admiring them too
I put my assistance for others
ahead of you and they left me.
I put others ahead of you and
pushed you away
Now I'm alone.
(179)

Oasis

In this world of rage and violence,
I've found my oasis
Surrounded by selfishness and greed
I have a sanctuary
In a world of bitterness and revenge,
I can go to a shelter
That place is kindness
That place is love
That place is you.
(180)

Objective

Learn the facts
memorize them
apply what you learn.
learn new facts
Memorize and apply
that knowledge
Growth is the objective
(181)

Pumpkins

From a tasty squash to a grotesque face
From a sweet pie filling to a mask to ward off evil
A seasonal treat whether for your tastebuds
or to shock you out of your seat
From pumpkins to jack-o-lanterns
they'll keep you jumpin'

(182)

Problematic

We want to be millionaires and to be famous,
but we can't quit the job we hate.
Working at the job while working for
our goal is too much to do
there won't be time to chill,
our lives will be too full.
Why would we rather work at a job
we hate instead of pursuing our dreams
because we can do half-ass work
at the job and still get compensation
but to get income from our dreams
requires us to be our best.

(183)

Peace and Love

Anger and rage are the enemies, bitterness and hatred are their allies
Love and peace give you the strength to overcome them tolerance and hope are your allies
Love gives you the strength, peace keeps you calm
Tolerance helps you to accept what comes
And hope gives you a positive outlook

(184)

Qi

Energy can't be created or destroyed but it can be transformed
Change negative energy to positive energy
Change lazy energy into active energy
Change low energy to high energy
Change what and who gets your energy
Change what and who gives you energy
Change your mindset
Change your thinking
Change your actions

(185)

Qualms

We haven't kissed
We haven't hugged
We haven't held hands
We haven't looked into each other's eyes
We haven't seen each other naked
We haven't made love together
We've only texted and Facetimed each other
We talked about a life together
Now that the time is here,
I'm having qualms about our engagement

(186)

Quest

So many regrets,
missed opportunities
and failures.
The largest regret is
not spending more time laughing
The biggest missed opportunity was
to travel the world
My enormous failure was
to let true love slip away
It is too late to regain what I lost
but I'm on a quest to enjoy the time I have left.
(187)

Rush, Rush, Rush

The populace is scurrying around in their busy little lives
missing the beauty that is happening
despite their existence
People busy themselves seeking money, fame,
and pleasure, sacrificing quality and elegance for speed.
The faster and cheaper a product can be made the better.
The longer a service takes the more impatient
the masses get, everyone wants things instantly and perfectly, with no waiting.
Rush, rush, rush.
Everybody wants to learn and understand everything
right now.
Understanding takes time, mistakes, and repetition.

(188)

Results Key

Someone giving you the answer to your problem
can be satisfying
But discovering the answer for yourself
is more rewarding and fulfilling
Working to figure out the answer yourself increases
Your understanding and knowledge
If you still can't find the answer
then ask for help, not the solution
For the most rewarding results research yourself

(189)

Reset Your Life

To reset your life
change your frequency
change your actions.
Start new habits to break old ones
Change your old mindset
Write down the qualities you want
To have and read it every morning
Everything takes time
don't get mad if you slip
make sure it doesn't happen again.
Reset your life for you
(190)

Six-word Stories

1. Sarah moved Jake sighed, finally divorced.
2. Sixtieth birthday Jamaican Cruise loving life.
3. One night stand now a dad.

(191)

Support isn't Being a Cheerleader

Sometimes supporting someone is more than just being
a cheerleader.
Sometimes you must assist them in working
Sometimes support is physical
They may need your knowledge
Sometimes they will need your presents.
They need more than lip service.
Sometimes words are not enough.
Sometimes you say you support them expecting them
to give up or fail but when they keep going you get irritated
Support is being a friend

(192)

Masculine Strength

Being strong you hurt,
But you learned how to cope
Being strong you prioritize
Your pain
and barely notice your gains
Being physically, emotionally, and
mentally injured, the trauma is accepted.
But you gain strength and wisdom
and can be the strength for others
(193)

Tired of Waiting

Tired of waiting for the right time
Tired of waiting for the love of my life
Tired of waiting for the right job
Tired of waiting for people to notice me
Tired of waiting for a pat on the back
Tired of waiting for good luck
Tired of waiting for life to happen
Time to take a risk and see where it leads

(194)

Tough Skin

People think stroking my ego is helpful.
They don't want me to feel bad
they encourage me even though my work sucks.
Lying to me and sparing my feelings
isn't going to help me improve.
If I suck let me know. I'm blind to my lack of skills,
I'm blind to the work I need to do
I can't see how I need to grow.
The only way I'm gonna grow tough skin
is by working through my weaknesses

(195)

Traces

Traces of lines in the sand
Lines made by feet, not hands
Made through the days and nights
Through hard and good times
Hard times that made me cry
and victorious good times
Times that had passed through my life
That made me stronger and more confident
Made love bittersweet
Love connecting souls
Connecting the lines that are my life
Lines traced in the sands of time

(196)

United

A ten-person team
Individual training
Individual strengths
Individual weaknesses
Individual doubts
Individual motivations
Individual likes
Individual dislikes
Individual lives
One mission
(197)

Until

I will be alone until
you come back to me
I will not hug anyone until
I wrap my arms around you
I will not kiss anyone until
I kiss your soft lips
I will lay awake every night until
you're lying next to me
Until our bodies connect
Until our hearts are reunited
Until our souls are one
I will be undone

(198)

Underdog

Achievements
are not a sprint
Fast Money
Easy success
Instant fame
They are a marathon
Slow money
Hard fought success
Delayed fame
(199)

Valkyrie

Guided you home with
Valor, strength, power, and hope
Now know love and peace
(200)

Vaccinated

Injected with courage to fight off fear
Injected with hope to fight against doubt
Injected with kindness to combat hatred
Received my booster shot of love to stay
strong in my daily battles
I'm fully vaccinated
(201)

Veterans

Battles small and large, in the home and abroad
Emotional or physical we all have scars
Fighting people or bacteria we must stay strong
Warring against a tyrant or for love
We are all veterans of some conflict
(202)

Where We Left Off

Hello, my old friend, I've missed your smiling face
how has your life been
Tell me about your adventures and the sites you have seen
I want to hear about the people you've met and the loves you've had
Talk of the fears you've faced and the things that
made you glad
Let's have a beer and pick up where we left off, tell me
about things you've learned I want to know your thoughts
Let's commune my friend and pick up where we left off.
(203)

Word Weaver

The paper is the loom,
the pen is the shuttlecock zipping back and forth
the letters are the threads that are woven
into a tapestry of words.
I'm the weaver of words
sharing the impressions and designs
of my heart and mind.
Crafting intricate shapes that I hope
will bring to life new thoughts and emotions.
The paper is the loom,
the pen is the shuttlecock zipping back and forth,
and the letters are the threads that are woven
into a tapestry of words.
Weaving words together building on knowledge
and experiences to allow the world
to see itself through the filter of my eyes and mind.

(204)

Which Way

Lost in this forest of concrete, steel, and glass
Surrounded by all kinds of animals
some docile and tame, some wild and ferocious
Which mountain should I climb,
where is a safe domicile
On what door should I knock
Where are the helpers, the ones who give directions
Which way do I go, where is my destination
my heart is looking for a home, but this world is so vast
I've combed my way through cities,
I've crossed so many paths
Searching for a place to rest my heart,
looking for a home for my soul.

(205)

Xanadu

You experience life every day,
whether the experience is good
or bad is your perception.
Life is hard but learning gives it value
Your greatest memories are the ones
you create.
Be intentional with spending quality time
with the people who matter.
To find a place of beauty and contentment
you don't always have to physically travel.
Sometimes you can find beauty in. your mind

(206)

X-ray

Like an X-ray machine can show what's in your body
I can see through your lies.
As clearly as an x-ray tech knows
what's wrong with the body
I can see the breaks, the blockages, the tumors,
and the deformities in your explanations.
The deceptions you try to get past me can be cured
with the truth, but you must make the decision
for the extraction.

(207)

Xerox

He is a copy, an imitation, a charlatan, a fake
He used lies to deceive you and win your heart.
He's not an honest man he just imitates manly qualities
He's only bold in a crowd
He's only tough when other men have his back
He only has courage when it's against someone weaker
He's a fraud, a deceiver, a manipulator
You will find in time that he copies other men

(208)

Your Mouth, My Mind

Your mouth says "Hi" my mind says that you like me
You smile and blush my mind says that you want me
You tell me about your weekend my mind says
I wish mine could've been with you
You mention the cold weather my mind says
I want to keep you warm
You speak of your lonely nights my mind says
I can keep you company
You pucker your lips my mind says, "Kiss her, now."

(209)

Young and Energetic

Being called "Sir," hits hard when you still feel young.
I thought of "Sir," as something you call older men
until I realized that I am an older man
I thought old was a feeling
but now I see it's the age of my body
I have grand thoughts about the future,
and goals I'm still working towards,
there are trips I'm preparing to take
and love I'm planning to make
My body is getting weaker, my joints are aching more,
but my mind is ablaze with excitement
about the things to come
I have a few more years, until I'm a senior
Some people I grew up with couldn't wait to be seniors
they looked forward to getting discounts
I wanted to stay young and energetic forever.

(210)

Years Gone By

I'm an old soul I always have been
Watching shows and listening to music that has long past
I laughed at black-and-white cartoons
Some were more white than black
My heart and body were young and energetic
My heart pounded as I raced and played with my friends
Those years have long passed now my body is old,
but my mind is still young
My mind still wants to go on adventures, but those years have gone by

(211)

Zigzag

The devices set in my path to
trip me up I've learned to
Skillfully avoid the traps
zig-zag around obstacles
Swerve around the pitfalls
turn to escape the setups
Sidestep the tricks
Dodge the foolishness
And continue to work
despite what's ahead of me
(212)

Zoo

I'm locked in this zoo, gawked at by the incapable,
inadequate, and lazy waiting for me to perform for them
Like a caged animal, I pace the floor, restless energy
surging through my veins
The smell of blood in the air,
the weak and the wounded just out of my reach
Ready to pounce attack and destroy
those who want to test my mettle
Those who want to fuck around and find out
the true capabilities of a beast

(213)

Z

A to Z ended
A challenge in a challenge
It was fun and tough

(214)

Acquaintances

Don't mistake an acquaintance for a friend
One will talk behind your back
the other will have your back
Friendships must be earned
through trust, loyalty, and your gut
Just because someone is friendly
doesn't mean they're your friend.
The Temptations said it best,
"Smiling faces sometimes,
they don't tell the truth,
they lie, lie, lie, and I got proof"

(215)

Don't Fit In

The movie Happy Feet is a perfect example of a society
trying to force someone to fit into their mold.
When he has something extraordinary to offer,
something that will not only change society but, the world.
If you're having a hard time fitting into society maybe
you're not supposed to, maybe you have something
extraordinary to offer.

(216)

No Need for Me

I accept the fact that these
young ladies don't want me.
They'll give me their time for a fee
All they want is what I can give them
They will only fill my life with mayhem
Movies have filled their minds
with delusions
Conversing with them gives me a headache
They believe that they deserve
a charming prince
too many stories and movies
have them convinced that they
don't have to change.
A man will come along
accept them with all their flaws
and give them the world

(217)

Where Have I Gone

Where can I be
Where is the artist that was me
Where have I gone
Did I get lost in this social storm
My language of flowers and love
The words that could make a girl blush
I would win the heart of my crush
Where have I gone
I'm lost in this social storm

(218)

The Chorus

A multitude of voices singing as one
Each voice performs as if it's the only one
I feel the vocals in my chest
I feel the words in my heart
I feel a change in my life
A multitude of voices singing as one
Each voice performs as if it's the only one

(219)

The Hawk

Her white feathers sparkle with silver specks
her heart is solid ice
Claws as sharp as razors
The beat of her wings sends a freezing breeze
She strikes everyone who ventures out of their abode
The winter hawk covers the city
Chicagoans know that layers are the only protection from this fowl winter season

(220)

Winter Rose

Roses are faded
Winter has me jaded
Violets are frozen
Temperature
is sub-zero
The wind is icy
Hot chocolate warms
us nicely
The snow glistens
Her heart listens
Nostalgic for when
we were young
loving, laughing, enjoying the sun
Now we're chilled to our bone
I hand to her a single white winter rose
We hold each other close
In the falling snow
(221)

Summer Dance

Hand in hand we walk along the beach
Sand and water in our toes
The cool water feels nice
Handfuls of shells just below the surface
We splash like kids
We dash and dance
Remembering past summers
And the ring I knelt to give you
Crying at missing our chance for love
The current grabbed your feet
The torrent dragged you away from me
The tide was too strong I couldn't pull you back

(222)

Overcoming

Acceptance is the first key
to overcoming Bad habits,
doubts, and fears.
Accept shortcomings, faults,
And bad habits,
conditions can be changed.
Then discover when
and how they started and work
on forgiving yourself and healing.
(223)

I Can Do it Better

Don't worry about those talking
behind your back
Those who say they can do
a better job
If they were more than
a dreamer they wouldn't
open their mouth
If they could do it better,
they wouldn't give lip service
those who talk about doing
a better job are looking for
validation
if they could do a better job,
they wouldn't need praise
Just continue to work
and press towards your dream
those talking behind your back
are not on your level and never will be
(224)

In Defense of "um"

A lot of people think saying "um" is a bad thing
they feel it makes a person sound less intelligent
But there are times when you need to take a second
to think before you talk. Blurting out the first thing
that comes to your mind is not always the best reaction.
Pause, take a second say "um" if you must,
of course, saying it too many times can
make you seem to have lower intelligence,
or something to hide but, you sometimes need
to take a second to think before you
speak don't be afraid to take that "um," second

(225)

Raise a Glass

Raise a glass for the soldiers
The ones who fought and
sacrificed for our liberties
Raise a glass for our parents
The ones who toiled and found
a way to provide
Raise a glass to the doers
The ones who stood their ground
even when surrounded by doubt
Raise a glass to the supporters
The ones who had our backs when
we doubted ourselves
Raise a glass to the lovers
The ones who make life worth living
Raise a glass for the workers
The ones who grind everyday
Raise a glass to the artist
The ones who beautify the world

(226)

What should I Write

What should I write
What should I say
Will anyone like my words
Does anyone read what I
write from day to day
What should I write
What should I say
Might anyone be entertained
Are my poems okay
What should I write
What should I say
Will my words give light
What should I write
What should I say
I must write every day
(227)

Capture Your Words

Capture your words don't let them stray
Whether they're bland or beautiful don't
let them get away
Capture your words so you don't forget
Jot them quickly and you'll be all set
Capture your words on paper or phone
Putting them down is like writing in stone
Capture your words don't let them float into
the ether
Writing them down to share with each other

(228)

A Golden Birdcage

A birdcage no matter how beautiful still puts a limit on potential
Some cages are in the mind, like a twelve-thousand-pound elephant being held by a rope
Other cages block vision, like the hoods placed
on hawks to keep them from searching for their prey
Most cages are generational, babies are taught
by parents to obey
Cages are hard to break free from, but freedom is worth
the effort and the possibilities are unlimited

(229)

Bad Things

I think bad things happen to good people so good people
can become great. So, the ones around them will learn that anything is possible
A high school football player lost his sight and was able to
play blind.
A surfer lost her arm in a shark attack and found the
courage to surf again
After dislocating his shoulder in the first half, the football
player played through excruciating pain and finished the
game with 229 yards.
Bad things happen to good people so their greatness can
be released.

(230)

Seasonings for Your Seasons

How do you season your season
The Halloween season is seasoned
with scary stories and candy
My season of giving thanks is seasoned
with family and football
My season of Christmas is seasoned
with gifts and laughs
I season the new year with toasts and
fireworks
I season Valentines with candy and kisses
How do you season your seasons

(231)

Organization or Company

NASA is an organization with a selected overseer
whose purpose is to make sure
the vision of the organization is fulfilled
SpaceX is a company whose owner
has a vision that won't be fulfilled
until after his death.
His issue is to find someone to replace him.
Someone who will work to fulfill his dream
when he's gone.
Being a privately owned company
there is more freedom to experiment
Being an organization they have connections
to draw the best skilled people.
Which is best for the world?
They both have strengths and weaknesses
they both contribute to the world's growth.

(232)

The Harlequin

They put on makeup to hide their flaws, and they dress
to enhance their feminine features
They appear physically weak, but their words and tones
capture the minds and emotions of weak men
They speak to him of desire, love, and marriage
to empty his bank account, emotions, and strength.
They take all he has, leaving him drained of energy
and resources.
The harlequin uses her looks and body
to drag men to their destruction.

(233)

Lonely Fans

Young ladies dance and show off their half-naked
and sometimes fully naked bodies
to lure lonely men to give up their money.
They don't have to have sex with these guys,
they just send them some nude pictures,
or videos and text some sweet things.
But men want more than just to watch.
They want a woman of their own.
There is no comparison between
fantasizing about being with a woman
and the actual experience.
These young ladies try to bring
that same gold-digger mindset into the real world,
and get shot down.

(234)

First Kiss

Our first date was at Navy Pier. I tried to look brave as
we rode the Ferris wheel, but my heart was in my throat.
We bantered as we walked along the promenade.
"I'm hungry, Stone."
"Okay." I said. Instead of going to a nearby restaurant
I led her to one of the boats docked at the pier.
"I thought we needed tickets. Can we just board?"
As we approached the deckhand, I pulled out my phone and
showed him a barcode for two tickets
"Why didn't you tell me?"
"Then it wouldn't have been a surprise." I chuckled.
Wrapping her arm around mine she pressed her D cups
into my arm.
When we descended the steps to the lower deck
I pointed at the buffet.
She gave me a peck on the cheek. After we had our fill,
we sat on the top deck to watch the sunset.
She gave me a peck on the lips and turned back
to watch the sunset.
I turned her face to me, I slowly leaned in
and pressed my lips to hers. We held each other closer.
As the boat pulled into the dock.
she whispered, "Take me home."

(235)

Chicago Weather

You never know what you will be exposed to,
Whether it's wet or dry, cold or hot
You know how to handle each one,
getting mad is useless,
whining is a waste of energy,
and frustration is not a good use of your emotions
You must bear it, and keep moving
Chicago weather is Bipolar and there is no escaping it.

(236)

Accepting My Demons

Everyone suggests that I should fight my demons,
but I've learned to accept them
They're part of me, deep down,
they often rise but I've learned
to not follow their words
They're the reason for my failures
by giving excuses to give up.
Angels are also in my heart,
and they come before I call
They give me the strength
to overcome the demons and the
courage to stand one more day.

(237)

Fear on the Rise

Fear is on the rise, "What if I fail."
What if I run out of words
What if I can't think of what to say next
Fear is on the rise doubt is coming in
fear is on the rise, but I can't bend
I must stand strong I must find a way
I must find the courage to say
"I won't fail." Not today
(238)

The plan

People would ask "Where do you see yourself
in five years?"
I didn't have a five-year plan.
I never had a vision that far ahead.
I was happy just to have a job.
I didn't care about a career,
I just wanted to earn my own money.
How much I earned didn't bother me until later years
I always had the idea that a high paying job
would come to me.
I never thought I'd have to plan and work for it.
I never knew I had to put in any effort
I always heard how good things just happened to people
I still don't have a five-year plan, but I do have a plan

(239)

New Sun

New sun
New moon
Same lover
New jokes
New day
Old messages
Same walk
Same hand to hold
Same feelings
Same lips
Same kiss
Same spark
(240)

Night Rider

Rose and I were co-workers. She dressed in the traditional yet professional goth-girl black. Black nails, black lipstick, her beautiful brown eyes highlighted in black.

We often shared lunch; she would talk about
her fondness for flowers, and I talked about
my passion for writing.
A couple of nights later we shared dinner
One Saturday afternoon she invited me to her house
for lunch.
She took to the garden in her backyard.
I was shocked by all the black flowers. She pointed out the
baccara roses, queen of the night tulips, black magic Iris, and her new prized purchase the night rider lily.
She grabbed my hand and passionately kissed me.
When I awoke, I was half naked tied to her bed and gagged.
"Hi, you will make a wonderful addition to my garden."
I pulled against the ropes. I thrashed with all my strength.
"Oh yes, baby keep it up. That's gonna give you some beautiful black and blue marks."
She slipped a blindfold over my eyes. I felt a sharp prick on my thigh.
When I woke up again, I was cold and damp, but my hands were tied in front of me. I sat up and ripped off the mask and just
when I tried to stand, shovel fulls of dirt were tossed on me.
I stuck my head through the ground.
"Hi, handsome." she said again, "Welcome to my garden."
That was the last thing I remember.

(241)

Walk with Me

Walk with me tell me your plans and dreams
Walking with you is what makes my heart sing
Walk with me let me hold your hand
Walk with me and let's dance
Walk with me this can be something steeper
Walk with me let's make this something deeper
(242)

Choices

We dream of the life we want
Not working towards that dream
we end up doing things that
surprise us
Trying to escape our troubles
leads us down a path
we never thought we'd take
We're young, we're happy,
loving, and friendly.
Struggles and lies make us angry,
and violent
We were open, talkative, and
compassionate but hardships cause us
to close off and be introverted.
Without guidance, we suffer,
without help, we worry, without
a hand, we get lost
The choices we do and don't make
affect the direction we take
(243)

Day in, Day out

Days of bright warm sun
Nights of clear skies and moonlight
Cool breezes and soft caresses
(244)

Birthday Girl

Another year has come and gone
Another year around the sun
Another chance to celebrate you
Another year I get to spend with you
Another opportunity to spin and twirl
Another dance with my birthday girl
(245)

Days

One person's day
of celebration is another's day
of mourning
One person's day of laughter
is another's day of tears
One person's day of love
is another's day of wrath
One person's day of hugs
is another's day of fights
One person's day of ease
is another's day of struggle
Whatever kind of day you're
having I'll either celebrate with you
or wipe away your tears
(246)

First Snowfall

The first snowfall is not snow
at all,
it is more like needles of ice
The air is frigid, the coldest
day so far
The snow can be beautiful to watch
from inside your home
But facing Chicago's snowfall
is another level of stress
Warm blankets, hot chocolate,
and hot apple cider
keep the cold from your bones
Trudging through the ice and snow
and surviving these freezing days
learning to appreciate the summer and the play

(247)

Your Goal

What is your goal
What do you want to accomplish
If you have nothing to shoot for then
that's what you will achieve
What is your skill or talent
How good are you at doing it
How good do you have to become
to reach your dream
(248)

Sneaky

I don't speak her native tongue,
and she doesn't know how
to express her points in English
so, when she argues
her words don't affect me.
I know she's angry, but I let her
meaning slip away.
(249)

Black Friday

Everyone bum rushes the stores
searching for deals,
trying to get that toy, that computer, that console
Everyone trying to please the one they love
by going beyond and above
It has become a tradition to shove, push,
and fight for that one gift
Maybe even end up in jail for a minor tiff
Black Friday deals are all a scam
to get you in the store
If you can't find what you want maybe,
you'll spend more

(250)

Regret

She teased him
He joked back
She smiled at him
He smiled back
He called her name
She ignored him
She turned when she saw him
He noticed but ignored it
He playfully tapped her arm
She said, "Don't touch me."
He couldn't tell her seriousness
And never spoke to her again.
(251)

He vs She

He buys groceries when he has an empty fridge
She buys groceries when she wants
to get out of the house
He buys clothes when he needs them
She buys clothes when she likes a style
He buys tools to have them when he needs them
She doesn't buy tools she pays a man to fix it
He learns to fight for protection
She learns fighting as an exercise
She keeps him fed and clothed
He keeps things working and protects her

(252)

Blue Moon

My days are colder
My nights seem darker
I don't feel heat from the sun
The moon has lost its romance
I have no joy
No reason to laugh
My smile is gone
I don't have the motivation to dance
The sun was a yellow ball of excitement
now it's just a lightbulb in the sky
The moon used to be a lover's light
Now it's simply a nightlight
lighting my path home
(253)

I Walk Alone

I walk alone in these crowded streets
I walk alone for many days and weeks
I walk alone because she's gone
I walk alone trying to stay strong
I walk alone on the hot sand
I walk alone without time to stand
I walk alone it's time to fight
I walk alone in my might
I walk alone on this dangerous path
I walk alone to face her wrath
(254)

Seeking Love

Love, is on a journey
Love,
is watching for an
unobtainable fantasy
Love, is looking for a man
who doesn't exist
Love, is wasting her life
seeking a man who has no flaws
Love, turns away from any man
who fails a test even, she can't pass
She says it is her life to waste.
Love, is seeking a love that's in her face
But her fantasy is blocking her site
(255)

Two Love Songs

You sing about your desires
I sing about what I have to offer
You sing about walks on the sand
I sing about a moonlit stroll
You sing about holding hands
I sing about sweet kisses
You sing about needing a good man
I sing of needing a woman to love
Our songs should be melded into one
A song about finding love
But our songs drive us apart
(256)

Weather Girl

Bright and sunny like when she smiles
Dark and cloudy like when she frowns
Gloomy and rainy like when she cries
Cold and icy like when she's angry
Fresh and aromatic like when she's
in love
(257)

Timing

Some opportunities only come around once
Rarely does life give a second chance
Fear causes missed happiness, missed love,
missed success
opportunity requires courage, action, and hope
Timing is everything in life
(258)

Boredom

You have a few choices when you get bored
You can either watch mindless programs or
you can get lost in your favorite past time
You can lose your mind in empty thoughts
You can lose yourself in designing your life
You can waste your mind on pointless talking or
You can grow your ideas in philosophical debates.
Boredom can be a reason to waste your life, or
it can be a catapult to your greatness
(259)

The Flag

We pledge our allegiance,
we salute,
we defend,
We show our pride,
We exclaim our pride
at the top of our lungs,
We hang the flag on our houses
We show our love for this country
and its symbol
We stand shoulder to shoulder
The blood, the sweat, the tears
we've sacrificed to keep the flag flying
We salute all the Soldiers, Sailors,
Marines, and Airmen
who gave their lives for the flag
(260)

Random Acts of Kindness

Someone may have had a worse day than you
Someone may be fighting back tears
Someone may be trying to find a reason to live
A kind word or a helping hand
may be the thing someone needs
to live another day
You don't have to be their best friend, but
you can be friendly
A random act of kindness can ease someone's
worry
A random word of kindness can soothe someone's
broken heart

(261)

The Victim

No one owes you anything:
Money
Respect
Time
Or love
Family may have made you feel special
but you're not
We all run late
We've all had a death in the family
We've all been cheated on
We've all had a bad day
Your struggles are the same as mine,
Stop looking for reason to ruin someone's day
(262)

Obstacles

One person sees an obstacle
as a reason to give up
Another person sees an obstacle
as a challenge to overcome
There will always be something
or someone blocking your path
You must find a way under, around,
over, or through
don't allow an obstacle to stop you
(263)

Boss Mind

A boss doesn't spend a lot of time
Dreaming, they plan and execute
They iterate and improve
A boss doesn't make excuses, they work
A boss doesn't whine about problems
They look for solutions
A boss meditates on advancement
They think about growth, about building
A boss doesn't complain about the work,
but he does complain about slow workers

(264)

Do It Hard

Success doesn't come easily
You must work at it
Despite how you feel
Whether sun, rain, or snow, you
must give your best
Through doubt, pain, and tears
keep pushing
Despite criticism, naysayers, and
Skeptics. Give your finest work
Starting at midday or midnight you
must finish the job
Success doesn't come easily
You must do it hard
(265)

Vibrations

Your words vibrate, whether
through thought or spoken
especially if there is emotion
You can change your world
and adjust your life.
You can go
from the gutter to the highlife
More words are spoken
out of anger or hate, which in the end
puts you in a cycle you can't escape
Your circle should be small and strong.
You keep each other
on the path as you move along
The vibrations of your crew should
be the same so all of you can gain
(266)

Treasure

The hidden thing, whether gold,
jewels, money, friendship,
or love
The thing that you search
for increases in value
the thing you desire
gives you direction
and focus
What is the treasure you're seeking?
(267)

One

I've been trying to get the job done
with the effort, the strength,
the power of one
We worked together there was more we
could do
we completed a lot under the power of two
We built higher than a tree we reached
for the sky with three
We constructed more floors, we towered
over others with the strength of four
Building together makes us, feel alive
we accomplished a lot when we became five.

(268)

The Story

The story of how I fell in love with you
is a conversation I must share with you.
I couldn't picture my life without you.
But with you, I had a sense of belonging
a feeling that I could be intriguing.
I wanted to make you feel the same,
I wanted to make your smiles gains,
I wanted to spend my days in your charms
and my nights in your arms
(269)

Steps

My top advancement,
publish four books of 275 poems
The next rung,
write 1,100 poems in 365 days
Next level,
write 102 poems in 34 days
First step,
write three poems a day
Making sure I complete
the micro goal
gets me to the final stage
(270)

Fight Failure

As I inch closer to my first milestone
giving up, creeps into my mind
I have three more milestones to reach,
and the failure mindset is urging me to stop
While building a finisher's power
the wall of failure stands before me
Using my pen is the only way I see
to punch a hole through this obstacle
Don't run from the barricade,
don't give in to the gate, but use my skills
and talent to find my way
(271)

When You're Young

When you're young you think you'll be young forever
When you're young you think you're indestructible
When you're young you think you're wise
When you're young you think
you have time to do everything you want
When you're young you think
good things just happen to you
When you're old you realize that
you wasted your youth
(272)

Faithful

You're not a failure if you don't succeed,
you're a failure if you stop learning
You're not a failure if you don't get it the first time
You're a failure if you stop trying
You're not a failure if you don't understand
You're a failure if you stop seeking answers
You're not a failure if you get tired
You're a failure if you don't finish
(273)

Finding Courage

Life doesn't change. I change.
I must accept the fact that I must stand up for myself.
Even if others will speak up on my behalf,
I must be man enough to speak up for myself.
If no one will listen to me
then I'll have to show them through my actions.
I will find my peace in boldness.
Everyone will not like me or what I say or do.
Everyone has their own opinion about things and people.
I must stand by my decisions

(274)

What Happened

He would get offended if another woman looked his way.

But now he's looking at other women.

She would get offended if another man said "Hi" to her. Now she smiles at other men.

What happened to the love and excitement, what happened to the promise to be there for each other

no matter what,
what happened to "I don't see anybody else,"
did the love just disappear, or are their faults
no longer cute?

(275)

Thank you for your support.
Please take a moment and leave a review.

Keep an eye out for the next books in this collection.
World on a String -vol. 2
Warm Weather Dance-vol. 3
Victory of Words-vol. 4

—

And my relationship book
The I Love My Spouse Journal

www.ingramcontent.com/pod-product-compliance
Lightning Source LLC
Chambersburg PA
CBHW020849090426
42736CB00008B/296

9798991954532